PRESIDENTIAL ELECTIONS

and Other Cool Facts

Third Edition

PRESIDENTIAL ELECTIONS

and Other Cool Facts

Third Edition

by Syl Sobel, J.D.

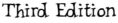

BARRON'S

To Izzy, who asked me to write this book.

All inquiries should be addressed to:
Barron's Educational Series, Inc.
250 Wireless Boulevard
Hauppauge, New York 11788
www.barronseduc.com

ISBN: 978-0-7641-4797-5

Library of Congress Catalog Card No. 2011934082

Date of Manufacture: November 2011
Manufactured by: M03I03D, Guangdong, China

9 8 7 6 5 4 3 2 1

Contents

Who Will Lead the Country?

Maybe you've heard grown-ups talking about "the presidential election." Maybe you've heard someone say: "This is an election year." Or maybe the TV news has stories about people "running for president." Did you ever wonder what the presidential election is, and why adults spend so much time talking about it?

You probably know something about elections already. Your school may have a student government or a student council. When you and your classmates vote to put someone from your class in the

student government, that is an election. When you and your friends decide whether to play baseball or play with sidewalk chalk, that's an election. An election is when people make choices by voting. Whichever choice receives the most votes wins. A system in which people make decisions by having a vote is called a *democracy*.

The United States is a democracy. Elections are how the citizens choose who will lead the government. For example, the citizens of your state elect the governor and the other leaders of your state. And the citizens of each state elect their U.S. senators and representatives.

The senators and representatives make the country's laws in Congress. The leader, or chief executive, of the United States is the president. The president's job is to make sure the government works properly and that the country's laws are enforced.

The president is also the commander of our army, navy, and air force. And when leaders of other countries need to meet with the leader of the United States, they meet with the president.

When the citizens elect the president of the United States, they are deciding who will lead the country. That is why the presidential election is so important.

The First Presidential Election Was No Contest

The first presidential election was in 1789. It wasn't really much of an election. George Washington was the only person running for president. He won. The same thing happened in 1792; no one ran against Washington.

Since then, there have been fifty-four presidential elections. In each one, two or more people have tried to be elected president of the United States.

The Rules for Electing the President

Every election has rules. The basic rules for electing the president are in the *U.S. Constitution.* The Constitution is the book of rules that tells our government what its jobs are and how it is supposed to do its work.

The Constitution has several rules about who can be president. They are as follows:

- The president must be at least 35 years old.
- The president must be a born citizen of the United States.

The Oldest and Youngest Elected Presidents

The oldest person who was elected president was Ronald Reagan. He was 73 years old when he was elected for the second time in 1984. John F. Kennedy was the youngest president ever elected. He was 43 years old when he was elected in 1960.

The Four-Term President!

Originally, the Constitution had no limit on the number of times a person could be elected president. Then, in 1951, the Constitution was changed, or amended, to add a rule that says a person can be elected to only two terms as president.

From the first presidential election in 1789 to the amendment in 1951, only one president was elected to more than two terms. That was Franklin Delano Roosevelt, who was elected president in 1932, 1936, 1940, and again in 1944!

- A person must have lived in the United States for fourteen years to be president.
- A person can be president for four years. That four-year period is called a *term*. The Constitution says a person can be elected to only two terms as president.

The Constitution also has rules about who can vote in an election. U.S. citizens who are 18 years old or older may vote.

There are also special rules about how to decide who wins the presidential election. In most other elections, whoever gets the most votes wins. But the Constitution creates a special system for electing the president. This system is called the *electoral college*. The electoral college is not a place. Rather, it is a group of people who meet together to elect the president.

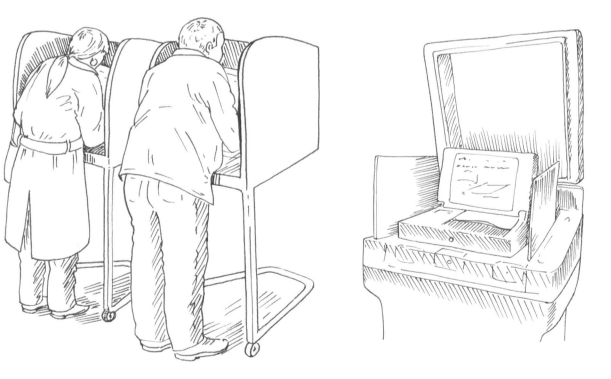

The Electoral College

The electoral college involves two elections for president. In the first election, citizens vote for the person they want to be president. These votes are called the *popular vote*. But the person who gets the most popular votes does not automatically win the election.

Instead, people called *electors* will vote in a second election called the *electoral vote*.

The people running for president, called *presidential candidates*, choose people that they would like to be their electors in each state. The popular vote in each state determines which candidate's electors will vote in the electoral vote. In most states, whoever wins the popular votes in a state wins all of that state's electors.

For example, let's look at a state that has fifteen electoral votes. Candidate Green and Candidate Brown are running for president. Candidate Brown wins the most popular votes in the state. Thus, the fifteen electors for Candidate Brown become the state's electors and will vote for Brown in the electoral vote.

Two states use a different system, however. Maine and Nebraska give two electoral votes to the winner of the state's popular vote, and then one electoral vote for each congressional district that each candidate wins.

The number of electors a state has equals the number of its senators plus the number of its U.S. representatives. Every state has two senators. The number of U.S. representatives in a state depends on how many people live in the state. Every ten years the government counts the number of people who live in the United States. This is called a *census*. If more people live in a state than in the last census, the state may get more representatives. If fewer people live in the state

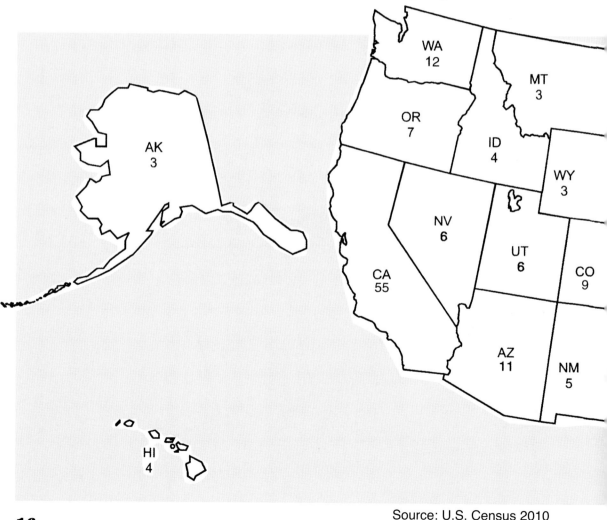

Source: U.S. Census 2010

than in the last census, or if the state has not gained as many people as other states, it may get fewer representatives.

The states with the fewest people have only one U.S. representative. So one U.S. representative plus two senators means they have three electoral votes. The Constitution also gives the District of Columbia three electoral votes.

The state with the most electoral votes is California, with 55. Texas is next with 38. New York and Florida both have 29, Pennsylvania and Illinois have 20, and Ohio has 18. The number

The Winners Who Lost!

Under the electoral college system, someone can win the most popular votes for president, but still lose. That has happened four times.

In 1824, four candidates ran for president. Andrew Jackson won the most popular votes. He also won the most electoral votes, but not enough for a majority. The Constitution says that, if no one wins a majority of the electoral votes, the House of Representatives must choose the president. The House elected John Quincy Adams to be president.

In 1876, Samuel J. Tilden won the popular vote. He also won the most electoral votes, but fell one elector short of the majority he needed to be president. Electoral votes in three states still needed to be counted. Both Tilden and Rutherford B. Hayes claimed they won the votes in those states. Congress picked a group of people called the Electoral Commission to decide who won those electoral votes. The commission decided that Hayes won those electoral votes, and he became president.

In 1888, more people voted for Grover S. Cleveland, who was president at the time, than for his opponent, Benjamin Harrison. However, the states Harrison won had 233 electors, while the states Cleveland won had 188. So Harrison became the president.

In 2000, Al Gore won more popular votes than George W. Bush. But Bush won 271 electoral votes, one more than the number needed to win the election.

of electoral votes a state gets could change, depending upon the results of the census every ten years.

After the popular election, the electors in each state meet to vote for president. Their votes are counted several weeks later in Congress. Whichever candidate gets a *majority*—more than half—of the electoral votes wins. Of course, everyone usually knows before the electors vote which candidate will win. That's because everyone knows by then which candidate's electors were chosen on Election Day.

The electoral college is a complicated system. The important thing to remember is that on Election Day, when people vote for a candidate, they are actually voting for their candidate's electors.

Why Is There An Electoral College?

The men who wrote the Constitution, who we call the Founders, argued over how to elect the president. Some wanted the people to elect the president directly. Others wanted Congress to elect the president. In the end, they agreed to have the people vote for electors who would choose the president. The Founders thought the electors would be an "assembly of wise men and learned elders." It hasn't always worked that way, but we still use the electoral college to elect the President of the United States.

The Presidential Campaign

Elections for president are held every four years. Here's an easy way to remember which years are election years: Election years always end in numbers that can be divided by four. The years 2000, 2004, 2008, 2012, and so on, are all presidential election years. *Election Day* is the Tuesday after the first Monday in November.

NOVEMBER

Sunday	Monday	Tuesday	Wednesday	Thursday	Friday	Saturday
		1	2	3	4	5
6	7	8 ELECTION DAY	9	10	11 VETERANS DAY	12
13	14	15	16	17	18	19
20	21	22	23	24 THANKSGIVING	25	26
27	28	29	30			

People who want to be president begin planning for the election very early, usually more than one year before the election. The period of time from when people first announce that they want to be president until Election Day is called the *presidential campaign*.

The first step in the campaign is when the major *political parties* choose their presidential candidates. Political parties are groups of people who share many of the same ideas about how the government should work. For most of its history, this country has had two major political parties. The parties have had different names. There have been parties called the Whigs, the Federalists, and the Democratic-Republicans. The two major parties now are the Democrats and the Republicans.

There have also been many smaller political parties. These are called *third parties*. Most presidential elections have one or more third-party candidates. Most of the time, candidates for the third parties get many fewer votes than the candidates for the Democrats and Republicans.

The campaign begins when people announce that they want to be the candidate for their party. Anyone who meets the constitutional requirements can be president. Usually, presidential candidates are leaders of the government, such as senators, U.S. representatives, or governors of states. Several candidates usually compete against each other to become their party's candidate.

Voters in each state help to pick their party's candidate. Some states hold *primary elections* to help select the candidates for each party. These elections are held early in the election year, usually starting in February. In other states, members of the political parties get together in a meeting called a *caucus*. The primary elections and the caucuses have the same purpose. Voters decide which person they want to be their party's candidate in the presidential election in November.

The candidates spend much time and effort before the primary elections and caucuses trying to win votes. Candidates travel from state to state. They make speeches, meet people at parades, picnics, and ball games, and appear on television. Usually, there are many candidates running for president in the first primaries and caucuses. By the time the last primaries and caucuses are held, only a few candidates are left. The rest have quit the campaign because they have been getting very few votes. They know they do not have enough votes to become their party's candidate.

Then in the summer, after the caucuses and primary elections are over, each party has a big meeting called a *convention*. The Republicans have a convention, and the Democrats have a convention. Sometimes, third parties have conventions, too. At the conventions, representatives from each state, called *delegates*, vote to choose their party's candidate. The number of delegates voting for each candidate usually depends on the number of votes the candidate got in the primary elections and caucuses. The more votes a candidate won in the primary elections and caucuses, the more delegates the candidate has at the convention. Sometimes the delegates vote several times until they pick a candidate.

In 2008, John McCain was nominated for president by the Republican Party. The Democrats chose Barack Obama as their candidate for president. Obama was the first African-American to be nominated for president by one of the major political parties.

Third-Party Candidates

The best finish by a third-party candidate was in 1912. Theodore Roosevelt of the Progressive Party came in second place. Roosevelt was a Republican president from 1901 to 1909. The president in 1912, William Howard Taft, was also a Republican. After the Republicans chose Taft to run for a second term in 1912, Roosevelt formed the Progressive Party. That party was also called the Bull Moose Party, because once, when someone asked Roosevelt how he felt, he said he felt "fit as a bull moose." Roosevelt got more popular votes and more electoral votes than Taft. But Woodrow Wilson, the Democratic Party candidate, won the popular vote and more than half the electoral votes, so he won the election.

Actually, the Republican Party started off as a third party. In the 1850s, the Whig Party was losing its popularity. A third party was taking its place. That was the Republican Party, led by Abraham Lincoln.

Conventions are very colorful, noisy events. They feature big bands, lots of balloons, and thousands of delegates, political party members, and their families. Some delegates and party members wear funny costumes, sing songs, and chant slogans to show how much they love their party and their candidate. The leaders of the parties give speeches, saying how much they support their party and their candidate. Sometimes, famous actors and sports stars give speeches, too. Finally, the candidates give speeches, saying what they would do if they were elected president.

The main purpose of the convention is to pick the party's candidate. But the conventions are also a time for members of the party to celebrate—and to show off their candidate to the voters. People watch the conventions on television and read about them in newspapers, magazines, and on the Internet. The voters learn about the candidates by what they say, and by what people say about them, at the conventions. The party members show lots of support for their candidates at the conventions because they know voters are watching.

Keeping It in the Family

Five sets of relatives have been president, including two fathers and sons. John Adams was the second president, elected in 1796. His son, John Quincy Adams, was elected the sixth president in 1824. George W. Bush was elected in 2000 as the forty-third president and reelected in 2004. He is the son of the forty-first president, George Bush, who was elected in 1988.

Benjamin Harrison, the twenty-third president, elected in 1888, was the grandson of the ninth president, William Henry Harrison, who was elected in 1840. James Madison, who was elected as the fourth president in 1808, was a cousin of Zachary Taylor, who in 1848 was elected as the twelfth president. And Theodore Roosevelt and Franklin D. Roosevelt were cousins. Theodore Roosevelt became the twenty-sixth president in 1901. Franklin Roosevelt, the thirty-second president, was elected four times starting in 1932.

First Ladies

Neither the Constitution nor the laws of the United States give any jobs or responsibilities to the president's family. But many of the wives of the presidents have earned fame and admiration for work they did while their husbands were president.

Some of the presidents' wives became famous as hostesses. Dolley Madison, wife of the fourth president, James Madison, was particularly well-known as the White House hostess. Indeed, even before her husband became president, she served as White House hostess for Thomas Jefferson, the third president, because Jefferson's wife had died before he became president.

Dolley Madison

Lou Hoover

Eleanor Roosevelt

Other presidents' wives have become famous for important work they did outside of the White House. Lou Hoover, wife of Herbert Hoover, was active in many organizations and served as president of the Girl Scouts of America. Eleanor Roosevelt, wife of Franklin D. Roosevelt, became known for supporting programs to help underprivileged people. Lady Bird Johnson, wife of Lyndon Johnson, was famous for making America beautiful. She helped to create parks in cities and improve the landscape along highways throughout the United States. Hillary Clinton, wife of Bill Clinton, was also active in many programs and causes during her husband's presidency. In 2000, as her husband was about to leave office, she was elected to the U.S. Senate from the state of New York. In 2008, she unsuccessfully ran for president in the primary elections. The following year she was appointed Secretary of State.

The president's wife has been called the "First Lady" since about 1877; that name was used to refer to Lucy Hayes, wife of Rutherford B. Hayes. So far, all of the presidents have been men. When a woman is elected president, what do you think the president's husband will be called?

Lady Bird Johnson

Lucy Hayes

Hillary Clinton

Then the campaign enters its final months. The candidates travel around the country. Big crowds of people gather to hear the candidates speak. Often, the families of the candidates travel around the country, too. Sometimes they stand on stage with the candidate. Sometimes they make speeches saying why the candidate would be a great president.

The candidates usually hold several *debates*. At the debates, the candidates appear together, answering questions and explaining what they would do if they were president. These debates are usually on television, so voters around the country can watch and decide who to vote for.

The news media, that is, the newspapers, radio, and television news, watch presidential elections very closely. They know that choosing a president is a very important event for the United States. They try to tell the people as much as they can about the candidates for president and vice president. This helps voters decide who to choose.

You will see many television ads for the candidates, particularly in the weeks before the election. Television ads have played an important part in presidential elections since 1952, when Dwight Eisenhower first used them. Those ads featured the catchy slogan, "I Like Ike" (referring to the nickname that Gen. Eisenhower was known by during World War II).

Finally, November arrives and it's Election Day. Millions of citizens vote in every state, city, and town in the United States. The votes are counted. The person who gets the most votes in each state wins that state's electoral votes. Even though the electors don't vote until January, everyone usually knows before then who the winner is.

The Winner Is . . .

The news media also try to predict who will win. The experts who make these predictions are often right. But there is at least one well-known time when they were very wrong. In 1948, Harry S Truman ran for a second term against Thomas Dewey. It was a close election. While the votes were still being counted, one newspaper, the *Chicago Tribune*, was so sure Dewey would win that it printed a front page story with the headline "Dewey Defeats Truman." When all of the votes were counted, however, Truman had won. There is a very famous picture of President Truman holding up the paper with the incorrect headline, with a big smile on his face.

The news media also had a hard time on election night 2000. Al Gore was winning more popular votes than George W. Bush, but the electoral vote was very close. Early in the night, the major television networks had said that Gore would win Florida, which looked liked a good sign for him. Later, the networks said that Bush had won Florida and declared him the winner of the election. Some newspapers prepared headlines saying Bush had won. But the votes were so close in Florida that they had to be counted again. The candidates sent lawyers to court, including to the Supreme Court of the United States, to argue about how to count the votes in Florida. Eventually, five weeks after Election Day, it was decided that Bush had won Florida and its electoral votes, and therefore had won the election.

The President Who Counts Twice

Forty-three people have served as president. But the United States has had forty-four presidents. How can that be? Grover S. Cleveland was elected the twenty-second president in 1884. Four years later, he lost the election to Benjamin Harrison, who became the twenty-third president. (Remember, that was the election in which Cleveland won more popular votes, but lost the electoral vote.) Then, in 1892, Cleveland ran against Harrison and beat him, becoming the twenty-fourth president. So Cleveland counts as one person, but as two presidents.

The person elected president does not take over right away. The new president needs time to select the people who will be advisors and help run the government. The new president's four-year term begins on January 20th, about ten weeks after the election. That day is called *Inauguration Day.*

Actually, the inauguration for George Washington, the first U.S. president, was on April 30, 1789. After that, Inauguration Day was on March 4 from 1793 to 1933. That gave electors from each state nearly four months after Election Day to cast their electoral ballots, which they needed during the days when most transportation was by horse. By 1933 transportation had improved and Inauguration Day was changed to January 20 by the 20th Amendment to the Constitution. That allowed the new president to take office sooner after the election.

What If Something Happens to the President?

W hat if the president gets in an accident or gets too sick to do the job of president anymore? What happens if the president dies? What if the president behaves very badly, and Congress decides to remove the president from office? (The Constitution says Congress can do that, but Congress has never actually removed the president.)

The Constitution has rules for what to do in case something happens to the president. The Constitution creates the job of *vice president*. The vice president's main job is to be the president of the U.S. Senate. But the Constitution also says that if the president dies, quits, is removed, or is unable to do the job of president, the vice president becomes president.

The vice president is elected at the same time as the president. Each political party chooses someone to run as vice president at the same convention at which it chooses a presidential candidate. Usually, the candidate for president picks the vice president, and the delegates at the convention approve the choice.

A party's candidates for president and vice president are called the party's *ticket*. That means that they are listed together on the voting ballot. Citizens vote for a party's presidential candidate and vice presidential candidate together. An electoral vote for the presidential candidate also counts as an electoral vote for the vice presidential candidate.

The vice presidential candidates also travel around the country making speeches. Sometimes they travel and appear with their party's presidential candidate. Sometimes they campaign on their own.

A vice president who becomes president must choose someone to be the new vice president. The Senate and the House of Representatives must vote to approve the new vice president. Once they do, the new vice president will become president if the new president cannot continue. The new president and vice president will do their jobs until the next scheduled election.

And what if something happens to the president and vice president at the same time? This has never happened. But just in case, Congress has made laws that give the order in which other leaders of the government would take the place of, or *succeed*, the president. This *order of succession* begins with the two leaders of Congress. They are the Speaker of the House of Representatives followed by the President Pro Tempore of the Senate. After that, the leaders of the government agencies that work for the president would succeed.

The Constitution and Congress have made clear rules so that there is always a president to lead the country, and that every four years the citizens can elect a president.

Order of Succession

1. Vice President

2. Speaker of the House

3. President Pro Tempore
   of the Senate

4. Secretary of State

5. Secretary of the Treasury

6. Secretary of Defense

7. Attorney General

8. Secretary of the Interior

9. Secretary of Agriculture

10. Secretary of Commerce

11. Secretary of Labor

12. Secretary of Health
    & Human Services

13. Secretary of Housing
    & Urban Development

14. Secretary of Transportation

15. Secretary of Energy

16. Secretary of Education

17. Secretary of Veterans' Affairs

18. Secretary of Homeland Security

The Vice President Becomes President

Nine times in this country's history, a vice president has become president. The first time this happened was in 1841, when John Tyler succeeded William Henry Harrison after Harrison died.

The other vice presidents who succeeded presidents were as follows:

Millard Fillmore, who became president in 1850 after Zachary Taylor died.

Andrew Johnson, who succeeded Abraham Lincoln after Lincoln was shot and killed in 1865.

Chester A. Arthur, who became president in 1881 after James A. Garfield was shot and killed.

Theodore Roosevelt, who succeeded William McKinley after he was shot and killed in 1901.

Calvin Coolidge, who became president in 1923 upon the death of Warren G. Harding.

Harry S Truman, who in 1945 succeeded Franklin D. Roosevelt after his death.

Lyndon B. Johnson, who became president in 1963 after John F. Kennedy was shot and killed.

Gerald R. Ford, who in 1974 became president after Richard M. Nixon resigned.

Here is one more thing for you: a list of all of the people who have been president, the years in which they served, and the name of their political party.

The Presidents of the United States

PRESIDENT	YEARS	PARTY
1. George Washington	1789–1797	Federalist
2. John Adams	1797–1801	Federalist
3. Thomas Jefferson	1801–1809	Democratic-Republican
4. James Madison	1809–1817	Democratic-Republican
5. James Monroe	1817–1825	Democratic-Republican
6. John Quincy Adams	1825–1829	Democratic-Republican
7. Andrew Jackson	1829–1837	Democrat
8. Martin Van Buren	1837–1841	Democrat
9. William H. Harrison	1841	Whig
10. John Tyler	1841–1845	Whig
11. James K. Polk	1845–1849	Democrat
12. Zachary Taylor	1849–1850	Whig
13. Millard Fillmore	1850–1853	Whig
14. Franklin Pierce	1853–1857	Democrat
15. James Buchanan	1857–1861	Democrat
16. Abraham Lincoln	1861–1865	Republican
17. Andrew Johnson	1865–1869	Democrat*
18. Ulysses S. Grant	1869–1877	Republican
19. Rutherford B. Hayes	1877–1881	Republican
20. James A. Garfield	1881	Republican
21. Chester A. Arthur	1881–1885	Republican
22. Grover S. Cleveland	1885–1889	Democrat
23. Benjamin Harrison	1889–1893	Republican

24. Grover S. Cleveland	1893–1897	Democrat
25. William McKinley	1897–1901	Republican
26. Theodore Roosevelt	1901–1909	Republican
27. William H. Taft	1909–1913	Republican
28. Woodrow Wilson	1913–1921	Democrat
29. Warren G. Harding	1921–1923	Republican
30. Calvin Coolidge	1923–1929	Republican
31. Herbert C. Hoover	1929–1933	Republican
32. Franklin D. Roosevelt	1933–1945	Democrat
33. Harry S Truman	1945–1953	Democrat
34. Dwight D. Eisenhower	1953–1961	Republican
35. John F. Kennedy	1961–1963	Democrat
36. Lyndon B. Johnson	1963–1969	Democrat
37. Richard M. Nixon	1969–1974	Republican
38. Gerald R. Ford	1974–1977	Republican
39. James E. Carter	1977–1981	Democrat
40. Ronald W. Reagan	1981–1989	Republican
41. George Bush	1989–1993	Republican
42. William J. Clinton	1993–2001	Democrat
43. George W. Bush	2001–2009	Republican
44. Barack Obama	2009–present	Democrat

*Andrew Johnson ran as Abraham Lincoln's vice presidential candidate in the election of 1864. Johnson was a Democrat and Lincoln was a Republican, but they ran together on the National Union party ticket. That party consisted of Democrats and Republicans who wanted to keep the country together during the Civil War. When Lincoln was killed in 1865, Johnson became president.

Conclusion

You have learned all about presidential elections. You have learned what the rules are to run for president, and what the rules are for electing a president. You have learned about the electoral college, which actually votes for the president. And you have learned that someone can be president for a four-year term, and can be elected for only two terms.

You have also learned about presidential campaigns. You have learned about groups of people called political parties, who share many ideas about what the government should do. The parties pick their presidential candidates using primary elections, caucuses, and conventions. And you have learned that every four years, on the Tuesday after the first Monday in November, citizens vote for president.

Along the way, you have also learned many other things about the presidents and presidential elections.

There is a saying in this country: Anyone can grow up to be president. Maybe, someday the president will be you!!

Presidential Birthplaces

Eight presidents have been born in Virginia, which is why it is sometimes called the "Mother of Presidents." The Virginia-born presidents are George Washington, Thomas Jefferson, James Madison, James Monroe, William Henry Harrison, John Tyler, Zachary Taylor, and Woodrow Wilson.

Ohio is the next most popular birthplace of presidents. It was home to seven. They are Ulysses S. Grant, Rutherford B. Hayes, James Garfield, Benjamin Harrison, William McKinley, William H. Taft, and Warren G. Harding. Massachusetts and New York each were the home states of four presidents. Massachusetts had John Adams, John Quincy Adams, John F. Kennedy, and George Bush. New York had Martin Van Buren, Millard Fillmore, Theodore Roosevelt, and Franklin D. Roosevelt.

The current president, Barack Obama, was born in Hawaii.

Glossary

Caucus: A meeting that members of the political parties have in some states to help choose presidential candidates for their parties.

Census: Every ten years the government counts the number of people who live in the United States. The number of people who live in a state determines the number of electoral votes that state gets.

Convention: A big meeting at which members of the political parties from all across the country pick their presidential and vice presidential candidates. Each party has its own convention to pick its own candidates.

Debates: Meetings at which the presidential candidates appear together. They give speeches, answer questions, and explain what they would do if they were elected president.

Delegates: The members of the political parties who meet at their party's convention to pick their presidential and vice presidential candidates.

Democracy: A system of government in which people vote to make decisions, and whichever choice gets the most votes wins.

Election Day: The day when citizens all across the United States vote for president. Congress has made a law that says Election Day is the Tuesday after the first Monday in November.

Electoral College: The system for electing the president. Citizens vote for electors in each state, and the electors vote for president. In most states, the candidate who wins the most votes in a state wins all of the state's electoral votes.

Electoral Votes: The votes that the presidential electors cast. The electoral vote determines who will be president.

Inauguration Day: The day on which the newly elected president begins the four-year term. The Constitution sets Inauguration Day as January 20th in the year after the election.

Majority: More than half. A majority of the total number of electoral votes wins the presidental election.

Political Parties: Groups of people who share many of the same ideas about how the government should work.

Popular Vote: The votes that citizens cast for candidates on Election Day. But the popular vote doesn't actually elect the president. The electoral vote does.

Presidential Campaign: The period of time from when people first announce that they want to be president until Election Day.

Presidential Candidates: The people who are trying to be elected president.

Primary Elections: Elections that some states hold to help select presidential candidates for the political parties. These elections are held early in the election year, usually starting in February.

Succession: If something happens to the president, the vice president takes the place of, or succeeds, the president. If something happens so that the vice president cannot do it, Congress has made laws that give the order in which other leaders of the government would take the president's place. This is called the order of succession.

Term: The amount of time that someone keeps a job to which he or she is elected. The Constitution says the term for the president is four years. The president can only be elected to two terms.

Third Parties: Because there have usually been two major political parties in the United States, smaller political parties are called third parties.

Ticket: The presidential and vice presidential candidates for a political party are listed together on the voting ballot. Citizens vote for a party's presidential candidate and vice presidential candidate together as one ticket. An electoral vote for the presidential candidate also counts as an electoral vote for the vice presidential candidate.

U.S. Constitution: The book of rules that tells the U.S. government how it is supposed to work.

Vice President: The person who becomes president if the president dies, quits, is removed, or is unable to do the job of president. The vice president is elected at the same time as the president. The vice president is also the president of the Senate.

Resource Guide

BOOKS

Bausum, Ann, *Our Country's Presidents: All You Need To Know About the Presidents, From George Washington To Barack Obama* (National Geographic, Washington, DC, 2009), 216 pages.

> An attractive and authoritative reference guide, loaded with lavish photos and illustrations. It contains profiles of each president, full-page portraits, fact boxes, and other interesting features.

Blassingame, Wyatt, *The Look-It-Up Book of Presidents* (Random House, NY, 2008), 184 pages.

> An excellent biographical and historical sketch of each president and presidential election from George Washington through George W. Bush.

Davis, Kenneth C., *Don't Know Much About the Presidents* (revised edition) (HarperCollins, NY, 2009), 64 pages.

> Entertaining guide to the presidents, loaded with fun and quirky facts while providing basic information about each of the men who has served as president. Each section also includes a timeline describing major milestones in American history.

Krull, Kathleen, *Lives of the Presidents—Fame, Shame (and What the Neighbors Thought)* (Harcourt Brace & Company, San Diego, CA, 2011), 104 pages.

> Detailed biographical sketches of every president, with emphasis on their habits and personalities as men, husbands, fathers, friends, and neighbors.

Wagner, Heather Lehr, *How the President Is Elected* (Chelsea House, NY, 2007), 112 pages.

> A history of the presidential election process that traces the changes from the original Constitutional model through the present. It describes the increasingly important role of political parties, organized campaigns, the media, television, and the Internet on presidential elections.

REFERENCES

The Encyclopedia of U.S. Presidential Elections, David C. Saffell, general editor (Franklin Watts, NY, 2004).

> Single-volume reference book discusses the candidates, major issues, and campaign tactics in each presidential election through 2000. Also includes campaign memorabilia, presidential portraits, and biographies of the First Ladies.

Presidential Elections, 1789–2004 (Congressional Quarterly, Washington, DC, 2005).

> Comprehensive reference on the candidates and political parties in each presidential election through 2004.

Scholastic Encyclopedia of the Presidents and Their Times, David Rubel (Scholastic, NY, 2009).

> A thorough account of each president, presidential campaign, important events, and prominent people that were making history during each presidency.

The World Book Encyclopedia (World Book, Inc., Chicago, IL, 2010).

> Excellent biographical sketches of each president, plus an overview section on presidential elections.

WEBSITES

The American President: Resources (PBS),
http://www.pbs.org/wnet/amerpres/resources.html
Portraits of the Presidents and First Ladies (Library of Congress),
http://lcweb2.loc.gov/ammem/odmdhtml/preshome.html
Presidential Elections, 1789–2008 (infoplease),
http://www.infoplease.com/ipa/A0781450.html
The Presidents (The White House), *http://www.whitehouse.gov/about/presidents*
Presidents: The Secret History (PBS), *http://pbskids.org/wayback/prez/index.html*
U.S. Election & Voting Resources (National Archives),
http://www.archives.gov/federal-register/electoral-college/links2.html

Index